Replenish The Earth
The Ministry Life Cycle

"Empowered to Minister"

By

Dr. Laura Thompson

Copyright, 2009

AMC World, Inc.

First published 2009

Copyright © Dr. Laura Thompson 2009
ISBN # 978-0-9720750-9-1

All rights reserved. Without limiting the rights under copyrights reserved above, no part of this publication may be reproduced, stored in or introduced into a retrieval system, or transmitted, in any form or by any means (electronic, mechanical,

photocopying, recording or otherwise), without the prior written permission of the copyright owner.

Formatted using Open Office
Printed and bound in the United States of America
www.amc-world.com

Acknowledgements

I would first like to acknowledge God my creator who took the time to create me, not just once, but time and time again. He didn't just leave me spinning on the wheel. He molded me, and shaped me in a way so unique, that the gift he gave me could only fit in my vessel. If taken out and given to someone else, the gift would come as a sounding brass, a tinkling cymbal or an uncertain sound. My parents, Levi & Desrene Thompson have been at the core of my creative awareness. They never put a damper on the discovery of my intrinsic talents and abilities. Instead they encouraged me to pursue all that was in me. As a result, they were often shocked at the manifestation of things that emerged from this empty vessel. God can do anything.

While there are numerous mentors I'd like to thank (and they know who they are), I instead would like to give thanks to God for all of the trials, troubles and tribulations I encountered on this path. For without them I would not have a testimony. They served to test my character and the witness of the Holy Spirit within me. Today, I am the victor of my circumstances & experiences – not the victim.

I'd also like to extend special thanks to a dear friend

who gave me the freedom to separate myself to God in order to produce this work. I really appreciate the sacrifice you've made during a very crucial time in your life and development. God who sees in secret will reward you openly.

I would also like to extend thanks and appreciation for the contributions made by Bishop Gladstone Royal, Mr. Floyd Muir of G & F Records, and Merlyn Ipinson Flemming of Emerge Me.

Replenish the Earth

The Ministry Life Cycle

By Dr. Laura A. Thompson

Table of Contents

Acknowledgements 3
Preface 9
Chapter 1 – Music & Arts Ministry Outside the Gate 11
Chapter 2 - The Debate/The Balance 37
Chapter 3 - Empowered to Serve 49
Appendix 54

Preface

If ministry is indeed a life cycle, then it functions based on business and the principles of growth. The concept of cycles assumes that each stage can be perpetual/ongoing. Cycles continue over and over. The idea that life is a cycle denotes that it has a continuing growth factor. It is not possible to have life without creation and growth. After a person place or thing has reached a certain stage in development, a measure is assessed. In fact, measures are assessed throughout the process to determine normal and abnormal growth.

Most of what is written is based on the culmination of experiences and or observations made as people stepped into ministry. It is important to be intimately exposed to ministry behind the scenes. As you read of testimony and experiences both seen and felt, the intention is to introduce varying and sometimes narrow viewpoints, which will become cause in the matter of readers to take an introspective look at ministry within their own lives.

To minister is an act of the heart and comes from love and sacrifice for the betterment of people and for the fulfillment of purpose on the earth. Before one can get to "ministry" a link must be established between purpose and the gift(s). This book focuses a lot on gifts. I've been blessed with several gifts, which I choose to use for the purpose of building the kingdom of God. My heart is toward the souls of men and what can be done to restore those souls back to God – creator and giver of life.

Chapter 1 – Music & Arts Ministry Outside the Gate

By now it should be clear that with the gate represents persons, places and things within an organization or governing system. And most times, this system is one that's set up by someone else. So outside the gate represents a new realm of possibilities, and thus a ministry here requires a very different set of business tactics to develop and administrate. This is another example where no one is out there showing you what to do and how you need to operate as a business structure. Did I say business structure? Of course!

People doing ongoing ministry outside of an organizational structure need a separate business structure. This structure may include the formal creation of an organization and a local business license (consider if your income from the ministry is greater than 25,000 annually). There are many websites, books, tax forms (Form 1099, Form 990, and Form 4369 to name a few), and laws that need to be reviewed depending on the type and area of ministry being served. The way one accepts donations, offerings, gifts and other monies should be tracked.

Distribution

There are plenty of ways to share your ministry with others off the stage. A person could provide recordings of him or herself that go beyond the workshop, seminar or message preached or the selection danced, sung or played on an instrument. So if your ministry sells products like books, CDs and DVDs or electronic files for download, there are certain entertainment industry principles that it should follow.

Before we proceed, it's important to note that the upcoming methodology comes from a do it yourself mentality. This is one that identifies some of the things one needs to get started. It also assumes that no publisher or label has been selected and you are acting independently as artist, publisher, or dancer without management representation. The business principles used are based on concepts exercised in the music and entertainment industry of which I am an educator and have been a practitioner of for over 20 years. They are not intended to minimize a person's gift or ministry to being just entertainment. Instead, the principles defined here are intended to assist individuals in the administration of their gifting and their ministry.

With this said, I will proceed. In ministry, it is possible to either have or obtain recordings of yourself – either via video or audio. There may even be an electronic copy (saved on computer or disk) of this recording. It is also probable that people in ministry create documents that can be converted to books, sheet music, magazines or other literature for distribution. For people that have a particular product (book, CD, DVD, electronic file for download), certain management principles are recommended which I'll mention in scenario form below.

In order to conduct commerce in the recording and publishing industries in the U.S., it is recommended that individuals first consider seeking legal assistance from an Intellectual Property Attorney. Here is a listing of a few things that may be required to legally do business.

- A Bar Code,
- A business license,
- Copyrights (forms from the Library of Congress)
- Publishing from a performing rights organization (PRO) (ASCAP, BMI, SESAC, MCP/PRS, etc.),
- An ISBN number for books,
- A registered trademark from the US Patent and Trademark Office, and
- An ISRC code issued by the Recording Industry Association of America (RIAA).

Depending on the type of ministry and the audience being served, one would need a certain combination of these items listed about. On rare occasions where a person or group is creating both literature and music for commerce globally, then the majority of the items listed would be required (in that case). With the advent of the Internet, global ministry is not impossible, especially for people in the younger generation or for the technologically savvy, or even for people that are surrounded by the technology. It may even be the aspiration of the majority of readers to reach generations of computer users through their ministry. This topic will be addressed later in this section. While this introduction might be frightening to some, there's no reason for alarm. Thus, it would be wise to proceed by discussing some of the industry basics through several scenarios.

Beginning Stages (1 – 2 yrs)

For example, let's say that your ministry is at its beginning stages. By this I mean that you've been asked on several occasions to minister in local environments. The results are profound and you get asked the pop question – "Do you have copies of _____ on CD or DVD?" Or you may be asked the question (as I was) – "May I have your notes? What you said was so inspirational that I want to do some more studying." To those questions, you respond with internal shrieks or horror and disbelief. What on earth do you do?

Well first, breathe. Say thank you and go home and pray. Then create a strategic plan that contains your mission, vision and objectives for ministering in your area. Next, if you have no copies of anything you do, gather as many tangible copies of your recordings, (audio or video) and immediately convert them to digital. In some cases, you may have to work out a deal with a sound or video engineer (such as give a donation) in order to get a copy of what you've done.

Copyright

This is the point where we begin making distinctions between the ideal scenarios and the others that exist in the world. At the moment the Creator imparts a new revelation to you in the form of an original work (something that did not exist before), then it is your responsibility to be a good steward of the gift you've been entrusted with. When you know that what you've been given is designed to bless people, and it has not been created in that way by anyone before who is still alive, then you my friend have a work that needs to be copy written.

The purpose of a copyright is to legally protect original works, which you intend to share with the public. Well, consider the possibility that the Lord gave you the impartation so that it could be shared. Whether or not you intend to sell this work in the future has no bearing on the point that the legal way to share duplicate copies or original works (in the U.S.) is by doing the following:

- Obtain a tangible copy of the work (convert it to a

digital file format to make your life a whole lot easier)
- Contact the Library of Congress – Copyright office in Washington DC (online at www.copyright.gov) and obtain the correct form for your music/sound recording or your literary work.
    - This option is relevant for works you intend to duplicate and share within the United States. There are different copyright laws for other countries.
- Complete the correct copyright form, get an envelope, purchase a money order or write a check for the processing fee (contact the Copyright office for the correct filing fee). Then in the envelope enclose the check/money order, the completed copyright forms and a tangible copy of your recording or literary work in the envelope, and with the correct postage, mail it to the copyright office.
    - The copyright can also be filed electronically. It would require signing up online with the copyright office, establishing a payment account, and submitting a digital file containing your recording or literary work with the completed and appropriate form, which can be completed online.
- The copyright office will return an official form to you within six months of the copyright submission.

Already there should be concerns about what you've just read, like what if you are not the original owner of the work and or how many works can you send in with one application, etc. The quick response to the first concern is this. When performing to music that you do not own, permission should be granted from the original owner, (in the form of a license) prior to the performance; and especially if there is intent to record and share this product as your own interpretation of the original work.

If the original owner is no longer alive, then you are free to copyright the work (music/dance) as an interpretation of the work written by the original author. By filing a copyright, you are being a good steward over the portion of the work inspired by God. In response to the second question, copyrights can become a bit expensive over time, so a person can file a collection of works together as one work (like a volume, series or chapters). It's most important to keep track of each copyright filing for future use. Whew, I've said a mouthful and this is just a very small portion of what you need to know to legally administer your ministry.

Publishing

Once your work has been copy written, it has potential

to just sit there and rot unless you've made plans to "go ye" and spread the good news. The vehicle/medium you use to spread/share the gospel, and the audience you intend on reaching will determine the type of publishing you need. The purpose of publishing is to broadcast your work simultaneously across the same or similar mediums. The publishing process gets your music or literature ready for distribution.

  A person has the option of getting a publishing company to set up licensing and distribution of the work or he/she could set up and distribute him/her self. Cost is a factor in either scenario. Of course I recommend the self-publishing option. See, when you make the decision to broadcast your music or message over the airwaves or the Internet, the broadcasting companies (TV, Radio, Internet radio, etc.) by law maintain business-to-business relationships.

  So if you intend to do business with them (in efforts to get your music or message on the air), then you will need to create a company who's purpose is to register the work with one of the Performing Rights Organizations PROs and then distribute the music across several platforms. The process is not that difficult but it will cost a little money to do the following:

- Go down to the county office and purchase a business license for a publishing company (which you can run from your home office),
- Contact one of the PROs (mentioned earlier) and

find out the fees to become a publisher (via their website, e.g. www.bmi.com , www.sesac.com, or www.ascap.com), and

- Obtain a username and password for the PROs online system. Then begin entering each of your works in the PRO's online system).

Choosing a company name is very important, here. For example, when I started my music publishing company, I did an Internet search on one of the performing rights organizations (BMI, SESAC, ASCAP) to see if the business name I wanted to use was already taken. I then reserved the publishing company name and opened the business in the same name of the publishing company. In music, membership with one of the PROs is important especially if the work you've done will eventually hit radio, the Internet or television.

The role of the PROs is to keep track of all broadcasts of the music from its writer and publisher members played over a period of time (on TV, the Internet, radio, etc). For each instance your material is heard or seen, a royalty is generated. The money comes mainly from the annual fees paid by churches, individuals, television and radio stations as well as Internet radio stations that graciously acquire a license to broadcast music/sound recordings before playing them. For each instance your music gets played or downloaded from the Internet, you (if you registered with one of the PROs) will receive a royalty from the PRO.

There are two levels of basic membership with the performing rights organization. You can be a writer member, a publisher member or both if you have a business. A music business with PRO functionality can mimic a record label but a few more things are required to make that functionality complete (e.g. a Barcode, a logo sent to the patent and trade mark office and affixed on copies of each product). I won't go into all of these facets because there are books that do a terrific job in describing the process.

To function as a true independent label, you would need to strive to become both a writer and publisher member. If you are the copyright owner of the work, then you can strive to become both the writer and publisher member of the PRO. Depending on which of the publishing companies you go with, there may be a cost associated with publisher level membership. But in general, there is very little if any cost associated with being a writer member. Being a writer and a publisher member enables you to receive up to 100% royalties (payments) from the broadcast of musical works you own or legally co-authored.

There are some similarities used for the publication of literature, but instead of looking to the performance rights organizations, the author must register with the copyright office using one of the literary work forms (like a TX Form). Here, the author would send in a copy of the literary work with the form and the application fee. Establishing a publishing business with your county office would be necessary if the author were planning to start a publishing company. In this instance, the author would need to obtain ISBN numbers (look up on google.com how to do this) and also get barcodes from the united code council (also known as GS1 – visit them online at www.gs1.org/barcodes).

There is however another option available with book publishing that can make your life a lot easier. It is also a form of self-publishing, but all of the work is done online and uploaded to a website. From there, a person can select the book cover design, upload pictures, etc.. It operates similar to a shopping cart, where items are selected from a menu and the user is prompted to make choices, upload content and then submit when finished. If this option interests you, visit Google.com and search for self-book publishing.

Barcodes in both the entertainment and book industries enable store vendors to keep track of your product's inventory. In the music industry Soundscan provides reports on which music and video products have the highest sales over various periods of time (weekly, monthly, etc.) The data from these companies ends up in industry magazines like Billboard Magazine, but is also available on line at www.riaa.org.

Let say for example that you want to sell copies of your

product online on one of the popular book or music stores like Amazon.com or iTunes.com. Amazon requires booksellers to have barcode and ISBN numbers to validate that it (the company) is dealing with a serious entity. Likewise and other online music stores report their sales number by publisher to places like Soundscan and to the performing rights organizations in order to issue royalties to the correct business entity. It would then be up to the publishing company (either you – the business owner, the record label, external publishing house, etc.) to take the monies earned and disburse them to the performers, writers and others that have participated in the creation of the work.

While not mentioned in detail, the creation and distribution of DVD videos would follow a similar approach to the music examples provided recently. The main difference is that where music is borrowed from artists and other writers, a contract needs to be created that details both the use and the compensation (for each song). While this may sound like a lot of research work, there is some good news.

There are companies that own song catalogs, which contain the majority of your favorite tunes. If you intend on using video as your means to minister, I would do the research to find the one or two entities that own all the songs you maybe interested in using. Then, when you go to your attorney to create a contract for use of the songs, you're dealing with one or two entities (cheaper in attorney fees on you), versus you having to create multiple contracts (more attorney fees) with multiple entities.

Bear in mind, the scenario provided above is just one of several ways to manage the administration of your gift. This method and many like these are mentioned because I strongly advocate a professional approach to the administration of your gift and calling. The technologically savvy want to receive data and information when it's convenient to them. Based on who your target market is, it makes very little sense to produce material in formats they don't utilize.

When I was younger, the Walkman™ was the portable device used with headphones to play music and messages on cassette tape. Later on, that device was replaced with the portable CD player. Portable CD players have been made obsolete by the advance of MP3s and iPods™. But those are still extra devices to tote around; so many phone manufacturers have incorporated MP3 and video technology into mobile phones. This is like purchasing a phone, a TV/movie screen, and a music player in one device. To take things a step further, the technology for music players have been made so small now, that these players are embedded in running shoes, toothbrushes and in microchips the size of a grain of rice, which get inserted in the forearm of individuals who desire this feature (similar to the insertion of a pace maker/defibrillator).

So there you have it...a mere fraction of what you need to know business-wise to get established in the audio, video and literary industry. I hope in some way the information provided, if anything helps to shed some light on the administration of your gift and calling. I'm sure it provided you with a lot of questions, which is a good thing. Before you do anything, contact an entertainment attorney, and also go to the appendix section of this book to see the listing of resources to help you carve out the best strategy for spreading your ministry and replenishing the earth. Recently I was asked to be a contributing author to the following industry books seen below.

David Baskerville, *Music Business Handbook and Career Guide* (9th Ed.)—*The New Music Business (Sage Publications)*

Geoffrey Hull, Richard Strasser, The Music Business and Recording Industry ISBN 978-0-415-87561-5 © 2007

Visualization

By now, your vision for ministry should be expanded beyond what is was when your first started reading the book. Hopefully you've gotten a glimpse of the fields and the harvest. Introspectively, an opportunity has been provided see your self and your ministry in a new light. Regardless of your age, there is still a place of significance for you in today's harvest field.

For some of you, life may be just starting for your and you glow with excitement. For other, the thrill of life is over and like the words of Evening Time says, you "sit on the side I look at the sky and wonder what I'm supposed to do" (Thompson, 2002). Wherever you are at this point, I encourage you to take another look at the ministry opportunities that you are presented with. Take a moment and look at what you've been given. Look at the technological possibilities out there and then ask the question, what does ministry look like spiritually today? Initially, it looks like nothing you've seen before. If you've seen it before, then it qualifies as status quo. (Sorry, but there's no fresh wind, anointing or fire in the status quo).

With this I am reminded of my hometown Boston, Massachusetts, where my dad loved to fish – every chance he got. He returned often to fish at one of his favorite spots near the JFK Library. On one of the trips we took back home, we were extremely disappointed when we discovered there were very few fishermen out catching fish.

Initially it made no sense to us. I mean, we stopped at the bait shop in Naponset Circle, picked up our bait, and got an extra line in case the ones we had snapped due to the weight of the 15 – 40 pound blue fish we had the potential to catch. We found our fishing spot and pitched tent there. Being the squirmiest person I am around worms, I was extremely still and quiet so I wouldn't scare away the potential fish.

With all that effort, none of the tactics we used worked to catch a single fish. The reason we were told was that the bay was being cleaned due the toxins in the water. As a result, the fish seemed to have routed to cleaner waters. And wouldn't it be a complete disaster if your intended target audience was no longer at the place they've been known to be due to toxins, updates or cleaner waters elsewhere.

Years later, I was told that blue fish returned to the JFK Library bay area. But with a maximum life span of 10 or 11 years, I am quite sure the fish that used to be in there left and never returned to that location. My point here is to note the glaringly obvious. The bait did not change. However most if not all of the intended fish changed. They changed with the environmental conditions. While we never returned to fish at the JFK Library before my father passed away, if we had returned, we'd have to do research on the characteristics of the fish in that same area today if we had any hopes of catching any of them.

During economic hardship or other factors, your intended ministerial audience may move or be on the move. They will move from the ordinary predictable life style and church style to something you've never seen before in order to adapt to the changing conditions. Like some of you, they will be outside of what's been typical – visitors attending a church service on a Sunday via an invitation or out of sheer curiosity.

If we ever reach a point in our society where visitors do not come to church, we will only minister to the choirs and the pews and the Amen corner – all of whom should be saved and on their way to glory.

Mighty moves of God happened without the gate - outside the normal realm of possibility. One example of this possibility was seen in 1905. At the height of the Jim Crow laws (http://en.wikipedia.org/wiki/Jim_Crow_laws) on racial discrimination people of multiple races came together at 312 Azusa Street seeking the Holy Spirit with the evidence of speaking in tongues (http://en.wikipedia.org/wiki/Azusa_Street_Revival).

On Trust and Money

Now that we have the ministerial and business aspects together, we will broach upon a subject that can make or break any ministry. Simply put, the subject is, Can God Trust you with Money? As your soul prospers, your personal prosperity will be positively impacted. Jesus said in Matthew, seek ye first the kingdom of God and his righteousness, and all these things will be added unto. Given that seeking is in order and the righteousness of God is in pursuit, what will you do with all the money and the prosperity that will come your way?

Believe it or not, this is another motivation check, so brace your self for this very short trip. While there are a vast assortment of topics to present from scripture and in life on trust and money, I will only discuss two that deal directly with replenishing the earth. The first is based on the life of Jacob.

Trust

Upon exiting the womb, he was known as a trickster. He had an encounter with God and his identity was recreated. At this point I'd like to stop and give thanks to our creator who has the power to recreate our identity despite what we've been known as. Being recreated as Israel, Jacob had a responsibility. When God establishes identity, he also instills responsibility. One doesn't just become a child of a king without being mentored about the responsibility with the name.

Today, many become excited about walking in the anointing but the sense of responsibility for that anointing can become lost without the mentorship required to understand the exceeding eternal weight of it. Being Israel, now Jacob had responsibility. It's one thing to be responsible for your family as a man or for your children as a woman, but when you have the weight of an entire nation on your shoulders, you might reconsider the approach taken in the past and go for one (an approach) that impacts the generations to follow.

Jacob quickly had to refine his charlatan ways in order to impart the identity and plans of God on his children. Could Jacob have known that his sons would become the heads of the twelve tribes of Israel? Could he have known that the words he imparted on his children and grandchildren would impact them for the rest of their lives and the lives of their future generation?

Consider for a moment the word of instruction God gave to you. Did it come in the form of a letter, a song, a message, movement in dance, a dream, or poetry? Who was the word intended for? Did the message get delivered?

Take a moment and jot down the instructions or impartation you received from God. Answer as many of these questions as they are relevant to your personal ministry. How did it align with his word? Who was it intended for? I know this question was asked before but it's time to become really authentic with what you hear and interpret as the voice of the Lord.

Just know that as you do everything your know to do in your heart for the king and for yourself, God will do as he did to Solomon and abundantly bless you. Is your trust in God holding up the outpouring of blessings destined for you? Better still, can God trust you to carry out everything he's asked you to do? When God asks you to do something are there things left undone? Are you a procrastinator or one that makes up excuses to doing what he says you should do? Are you responsible for holding up your own blessings because of disobedience?

The blessings of the Lord maketh rich and addeth no sorrow. Look honestly at yourself, where you are and your environment. Has obedience to God's command provided you with where you are today or did your arrive at your circumstances as a result of not fully trusting God and carrying out to the letter, what he said you should do. Again, King Solomon did everything he knew in his heart to do for God and for his house. Then God blessed him abundantly.

If we've fallen off the path, it's not to late to ask God to search us and know our hearts, try us and know our thoughts and to see if there is any wicked way in us and purge us from all unrighteousness (Psalms 51). Once we repent, we then need to turn from the path we are on and get back on the correct path. Only then can we serve the Lord with gladness and come before his presence with singing (Psalms 100). This in turn enables God to present us faultless before the presence of his glory with exceeding joy. See, we don't have to live in the land where the thief comes to steal kill and destroy. Obedience to God enables us to live the life he came to give us – and that more abundantly. But it all stems from the question that started this section. Can God Trust You?

Replenishing the earth is not so much about your personal legacy. Jacob instructed his son Joseph to write and become educated. Reading and writing were the skills that moved Joseph from the pit to the palace. Joseph became the heir responsible for telling the story of his family and who father Abraham was. Despite the trouble Joseph went through, he remembered his God and passed His goodness down through the generations. It is the goodness of the Lord that we replenish the earth with – not our own works. The work we do will eventually perish if not done for the Lord. The book of Psalms says it best.

> *"Oh my people, listen to my teaching. Open your ears to what I am saying, for I will speak to you in a parable. I will teach you hidden lessons from our past – stories we have heard and know, stories our ancestors handed down to us. We will not hide these truths from our children but will tell the next generation about the glorious deeds of the Lord. We will tell of his power and mighty miracles he did. For he issued his decree to Jacob; he gave his law to Israel. He commanded our ancestors to teach them to their children, so the next generation might know them – even the children not yet born – that they in turn might teach their children.* **So each generation can set its hope anew on God,** *remembering his glorious miracles and obeying his commands. Then they will not be like their ancestors – stubborn, rebellious, and unfaithful, refusing to give their hearts to God."*

Psalm 78: 1-8

When you take to the stage, can God trust you to proclaim His glory or will you invoke God's presence so that you can get attention? His glory will not be shared with another. I strongly encourage you to really and sincerely praise God. Don't ego trip looking for opportunities for people to praise you for the works you've done. A person may be skilled at getting people to really worship, but if the purpose of praising God ever becomes twisted in your mind, thought or deed, WATCH OUT. Pride comes before destruction and a haughty look before a fall.

I leave you again with this question: Can God trust you?

Money – Passing the Gehazi Test

2 Kings 5:20-27 (The Message Version)

19-21 Elisha said, "Everything will be all right. Go in peace."

But he hadn't gone far when Gehazi, servant to Elisha the Holy Man, said to himself, "My master has let this Aramean Naaman slip through his fingers without so much as a thank-you. By the living God, I'm going after him to get something or other from him!" And Gehazi took off after Naaman.

Naaman saw him running after him and jumped down from his chariot to greet him, "Is something wrong?"

22 "Nothing's wrong, but something's come up. My master sent me to tell you: 'Two young men just showed up from the hill country of Ephraim, brothers from the guild of the prophets. Supply their needs with a gift of 75 pounds of silver and a couple of sets of clothes.'"

23 Naaman said, "Of course, how about a 150 pounds?" Naaman insisted. He tied up the money in two sacks and gave him the two sets of clothes; he even gave him two servants to carry the gifts back with him.

24 When they got to the fort on the hill, Gehazi took the gifts from the servants, stored them inside, then sent the servants back.

25 He returned and stood before his master. Elisha said, "So what have you been up to, Gehazi?"

"Nothing much," he said.

26-27 Elisha said, "Didn't you know I was with you in Spirit when that man stepped down from his chariot to greet you? Tell me, is this a time to look after yourself, lining your pockets with gifts? Naaman's skin disease will now infect you and your family, with no relief in sight."

Gehazi walked away, his skin flaky and white like snow.

This story is presented in its entirety after the section on trust because trust is a factor when dealing with God and ministry. In a nutshell there is a time in ministry to be a receiver and there is a time to be a giver. God controls the times. The times are random and have nothing to do with the principles surrounding pride. For example, when you have been a blessing to someone they have several options. They could plant a seed (gift, financial blessing, etc) into your life, where their personal return can be 30, 60 or 100 fold or more. They could put the money in the bank with the interest rate is very low. Or they could eat their seed or bury it.

Just based on the principles of financial investment and simple math, I say option one is a good one for anyone that received a blessing from your ministry. Now what you do with the money is up to you. But the self-righteous stance has to die because it's based on the principles of pride. God, please help us to truly be receivers of your blessings. Help us to stop playing God. Amen!

Even if you are the richest most affluent person in the world, God gives you a heart to be a giver and a receiver. Now already I can tell that at least 50% of the readers have no problem with receiving. Some of us however have issues with the giving principle. When the Lord instructs us to give, we must not hesitate to do so, and that with a happy spirit. Even when you know there is a need, God is the supplier of the need not you.

When we use our thought to determine what should happen as Gehazi did, we play the roll of God, as if he doesn't know all things. Every time we fail to follow the Lord – especially when it comes to money, we function in rebellion. In the New Testament, Judas struggled with Jesus' ministry on earth. Judas had a hidden agenda. He wanted a revolution with Jesus as the head of the revolution.

Many will see your ministry and have ideas about who you should be and what you can do and how big your ministry will be if you do things their way. But does God want? God wants submission to his will – no tricks, no ideas, and no worthy causes created by you to use the money he told you to give away. There has to be balance – in our hearts as it relates to trust and money in ministry.

ASSESSMENT/STUDY QUESTIONS:

Write a list of questions you have regarding publishing and copyrights. Then relate those questions to your area in music and arts ministry. Develop a map plotter with categories that align with the copyright and publishing questions you listed.

Chapter 2 - The Debate/The Balance

To be Paid or Not to be Paid

This is the final frontier to be conquered in this book. This subject is brought up time and time again during workshops I do on ministry. In general it seems that some are so aloof to the aspects of money, resources, and ministry that they walk around looking broke and dusty as if they are still living in Jesus' day. If I were a sinner, I might consider running away from someone presenting Christ to me in that way.

Nothing about looking broke and dusty is attractive or alluring to me. Needless to say, each person has a perspective of what looks healthy, attractive, successful and admirable. God made us all differently. I honestly believe that God created specific evangelists with a particular gift to reach each person where they are the way they need to be reached, touched and inspired. There are also multifaceted people that can reach people on numerous levels in multiple environments.

There is something attractive about a successful person in ministry doing all they know to do for God. Does this equate to money? Some times it does actually equate to money because God takes care of his children. It solely depends on who the individual is and where their struggles lie. For example, there are people that know how to receive. They are good givers and they don't think twice about giving it all away if the Lord instructs them to do so. They are not stuck on money. Their generosity and clear heart enables money and resources to be stuck on them, so they freely give as they've received.

Of course you have some that struggle with giving. They hoard what they have. They find themselves bound in systems that produce pay or some resource to keep them. Some of them are motivated to serve by the dollar, the ten, the fifty, the hundred, the thousand, the car, the incentive package and whatever else they could get their hands on.

For these people, sometimes being paid can minimize growth and potential – leaving them stuck in the place where they're consistently paid. Sounds strange? In this case, payment a characteristic enabling people to execute the same behavior pattern. They're motivated by something external. After a while, the wave of the 'carrot stick' will have very little if any effect on performance.

When people are fed up and they want out a vicious cycle, no pay is enough to keep them. Why do people making six figure salaries want to leave a company/organization they've been loyal to? Usually it's because they're tired of being in a cycle doing what they've been doing and they want a change.

Even changes in atmosphere require the use of different muscles that have not been used before. Exercising these muscles will eventually enable them to grow and sustain the atmospheric pressures. While I agree (with all my heart) that a workman is worthy of his hire (Matthew 10:10) and people are deserving of the fruits of their labor (Psalm 128:2), where does pay come into the picture? It depends on your internal motivation (assuming there is something internal that can be motivated). The answer to the question depends solely on where you are in ministry and the state of your heart.

To proceed, we will discuss two more perspectives that relate to the preparation for ministry outside of an organizational structure. I've found over the years that many want to do ministry outside but have been deceived in the way to make this happen. Others have made people in ministry wrong for receiving money. And the debate continues.

Biblical Perspective

Our first view comes from the Message version of Matthew 10: 9 – 11, 16. Here an approach to ministry is discussed and has been adopted today by many. Consequently, others using this same scripture have condemned many in the ministry. So don't become shocked if others using this scripture misinterpret your ministry administration.

> 9-10 "Don't think you have to put on a fund-raising campaign before you start. You don't need a lot of equipment. You are the equipment, and all you need to keep that going is three meals a day. Travel light.

> 11 "When you enter a town or village, don't insist on staying in a luxury inn. Get a modest place with some modest people, and be content there until you leave.

> 16 "Stay alert. This is hazardous work I'm assigning you. You're going to be like sheep running through a wolf pack, so don't call attention to yourselves. Be as cunning as a snake, inoffensive as a dove.

Years ago, most ministries followed this methodology of modesty when doing ministry outside of the local church. I heard the gross interpretation of this scripture at times coupled with being poor in spirit (one of the beatitudes, Matthew 5). Anything extravagant was seen as having a ministry with no humility.

With this format for ministry also came a lack of organization when going out to minister. They totally trust God and expect everyone to be on the same page as them. When they show up to minister, they discover that there were practical things that needed to be taken care of and that everyone is not on the same page. In fact, when you minister outside the gate, there are certain things that the people expect you to take care (some of them were mentioned in the Music Ministry Life cycle section). Bottom line this approach is totally based on where you are in ministry.

Our next approach is seen in the ministry of Paul, the tent maker.

Acts 18:1-3 (Amplified Bible)

1 AFTER THIS [Paul] departed from Athens and went to Corinth.

2 There he met a Jew named Aquila, a native of Pontus, recently arrived from Italy with Priscilla his wife, due to the fact that Claudius had issued an edict that all the Jews were to leave Rome. And [Paul] went to see them,

3 And because he was of the same occupation, he stayed with them; and they worked [together], for they were tentmakers by trade.

This scripture is used as the model for missions based ministry. (http://www.globalopps.org/faq/index.htm) Here, the individual works in a trade/occupation that is in alignment with their ministry. Through the money made from this venture, the individual has more control with the budgeting and planning ministry based or mission trips.

Some may review both perspectives calling the first one welfare and the second an entrepreneur based ministry model. Of course the possibility of people taking sides exists within that assessment (The welfare group versus the entrepreneur group). As such, it is expected that the welfare group would have contention in ministry with the entrepreneur-based group. To some, ministries should not have a profit. To others, ministries should not have a deficit.

Which is the best model to follow? Follow the one that God tells you to follow for the area, environment and time you are ministry. There is no one answer or v iewpoint. The best stance to take is dependent on who you are, where you are and where you are going in ministry.

Location, Location, Location

The objective of this section is to get a clear harvest picture of where you are in music & arts ministry; To provide you with tools to minister effectively where you are; To empower you for ministering in music & arts outside the gate.

> And the LORD God called unto Adam, and said unto him, Where art thou?
>
> **Genesis 3:9**

One of the most important positions to consider in life is that of location. Location determines where a person, place or thing resides, is going, or is coming from. Soon after God gave him identity, assigned him his task on earth, the resources to do the job, gave him a help meet to assist him, Adam could not be found. He just took off behind the bushes.

A similar scenario is seen with in I Kings 19:4, where after his identity is known throughout the land (as a servant of the most high God), and he won a magnificent battle against the prophets of Baal, Elijah takes off and hides under a juniper tree.

We find another circumstance where Jonah has the mandate to preach the gospel to Nineveh but instead he takes off on a boat headed for Tarshish. Well that boat ride ended in disaster, as Jonah made a stop in the belly of a large fish. What is the prophetic anointing doing in the belly of an animal when we were designed from the beginning to have dominion over the birds of the air the fish of the sea? Specifically, the original intention God laid out for us from the beginning reads like this:

> And God said, Let us make man in our image, after our likeness: and let them have dominion over the fish of the sea, and over the fowl of the air, and over the cattle, and over all the earth, and over every creeping thing that creepeth upon the earth (Genesis 1: 26).

Then he continued:
> And God blessed them, and God said unto them, Be fruitful, and multiply, and replenish the earth, and subdue it: and have dominion over the fish of the sea, and over the fowl of the air, and over every living thing that moveth upon the earth (Genesis 1:28).

Son or daughter of Adam, where are you today? How far are you away from God's original intention for you? Some have the motivation and the direct mentorship, but lack the mobility to go and actualize what they were destined to do. Some have been deceived or mislead. And then again, some are just disheartened by the current conditions and see no way to make a real impact. Regardless of where you are, God's mandate still stands. Be fruitful, multiply and replenish the earth. Don't let the cares of life that exist on this earth overtake you. You were designed from the beginning to subdue or to control it! From my observation, I've seen a role reversal that represents the complete opposite of God's intentions.

This role reversal is just a mindset and it is temporary. It will not last. Once the light of God's word shines and continues to shine through the dark places of your life, you will soon see that God's word stands and no weapon formed against is designed to prosper. All weapons formed against you are designed to fail – from the beginning. So while there are weapons and there is deceit, they are not designed to pull down strongholds because these weapons are carnal. Through the word of God we alter our thought and our language because his word is the weapon designed from the beginning to pull down strongholds and cast down every imagination that attempts to exalt itself against the knowledge of God. Don't be susceptible to deception, but be sure that you are endued with power from God. You have the power. It's not just a mental exercise. Both life and death is in the power of the tongue. The power is in your language so that through speaking you can (as God did) declare that the earth is the Lord's the fullness thereof, the world and they that dwell therein.

Son or daughter of Adam, where art thou? Where every you've fallen off, you can be found by the omnipresent God of the universe. He designed your identity and calls you out to be who you were destined to be. You were destined to be fruitful. You were destined to multiply. You were destined to replenish the earth. You were destined to subdue things that were out of control on this earth.

(Read this aloud).

"Today I speak a word of hope and assurance knowing that Jesus is mine. I acknowledge that there is a lie going around that says I have no power or authority. But I know without a doubt that lie has no bearing on me because greater

is he that is in me than he that is in the world. While the silence of the lamb is killing the earth, today I speak knowing that according to Romans 8:19, the whole earth waits in anticipation for the manifestation of the sons of God. Without the word from God, the earth is still without form, it's void, and darkness covers the face of the deep. So with the authority God gave me from the beginning I speak light into the dark places of my life. Let the light of God's word enter the areas that lack form.

I speak a word of life that will bring forth organization and structure to the conformity that withholds me from standing out and the deformity that surrounds me making me appear helpless. I speak light into the lie appear to make my life and ministry null and void so that it (the lie) will be exposed for what it is. My assignment is not cancelled. I decree and declare that I have a charge to keep and a God to glorify, and that according to John 9:4 that I must work the work of Him who sent me, while it is day.

May the Lord equipment me with His power today and every day, to effectively minister in the dark places, and beyond my surroundings. And now with the knowledge of the light of God and with the identity and purpose He instilled within me, I am fruitful. I have the seed of multiplicity. I am equipped and empowered to replenish the earth. By the grace of God and the power of the anointed one and his anointed, I will subdue the earth and through the word, lead captivity captive (hold captive those that held us captive) (Ephesians 4:8), knowing that according to Matthew 18:18, whatever I bind on earth will be bound in heaven and whatever I loose on earth will be loosed in heaven, in Jesus Name, Amen."

Read this over several times today and throughout the upcoming weeks. Let the word of God and the Spirit of God find you wherever you are and restore you to your rightful place in him. Moreover, maintain the authority he has given you to replenish and subdue the earth.

ASSESSMENT/STUDY QUESTIONS:

- Create a payment structure/model for what things you think needs/requires reimbursement in ministry (either your personal ministry or some other music and arts ministry form).
- Why are there still issues with money today?

What part of the ministry life cycle is most impacted by issues with money? Please explain.

Chapter 3 - Empowered to Serve

Final Assessment

We've reached the final stop on a very powerful journey inward – to find the inner you. What a great journey it has been and I've enjoyed process with you. On the quest to find out where you are, you may be a pastor, evangelist, a retired person or a new convert. Depending on who you are, at the moment, your ministry aspirations may fit one the following categories:

1. Not in position currently (Available, but not being used)
2. Being used locally but considering venturing out/a new venture
3. Doors opened to new venture out but not out yet
4. Currently venturing outside of organizational structure in ministry

After looking at this list, and reading the contents of this book I'm sure God has inspired, and in some ways, re-empowered you for service. It's not over yet. In some cases, it (your ministry) hasn't even begun to actualize its full potential.

Habakkuk 2: 1 – 2 describes a man that stood upon his watch and waited.

We don't know how long he waited, but soon after it was time to write what he saw, making it understandable. This enabled others who read it to run. Habakkuk was functioning with an inward motivation when he stood upon his watch and then wrote. Mobility is achieved when others can run with purpose after reading and understanding what was written.

Without alignment, it becomes increasingly difficult to not only fulfill one's purpose for living, but to also reproduce, and replenish the earth. Through the ideas of this book, the goal was to inspire you to greatness and empower you to reach your highest potential in God, and to equip you with the tools needed to minister effectively. Maintaining relevance is crucial to your ministry not becoming extinct.

Final Thoughts

My father passed away in April 2008. Since then, many have been inspired not to quit but to continue on in pursuit of purpose. The legacy of his ministry lives on in me and in the lives of others he's touched. Some have been empowered to serve in various aspects of ministry. While others were inspired to serve in missions and in the community through food pantries, education and even establishing community gardens – planting where he planted. The overwhelming impact of his life inspired a friend of mine to write the following poem seen below.

I heard the word that a loved-one has gone, leaving this earth to be with the Lord. Hearts fell to the ground and many tears were shed, as the news of a servant's pressing and gasping up to the last breath.

I heard the word that a loved-one has gone, leaving this earth to be with the Lord. In the midst of mourning, the Lord came to me and showed me a vision not of sorrow, but of VICTORY.

In my vision, I saw God with outstretched hands saying to his servant, STOP LEVI, for it is time. In my vision, I saw God with so much love began shedding tears with outpouring rain from above. In my vision, I saw God with a smiling heart saying to his servant Levi, no need to worry you've served well, you've done your part. And in that moment, God provided a view to his servant Levi, of what he has sewn.

He said now Levi, I know of your fear of leaving behind your loved-ones whom you hold dear, but take a look at the legacy you've left as many gathered together because of your death. These are those who may have strayed from home, these are those who stuck it through the bad & the good. These are those whom you may have never seen before for they are from the seeds that you have sown.

So Levi, I bid you welcome to NO more pain No more

suffering and no more tears. And as I have promised through the many prayers rendered by you I will share with you what I will do.

To your family, I will provide them with renewed strength, enrich them with courage and with good health. To the church that you've served so well I'll ensure your seeds are nourished & will continue to spread your legacy shall live and shall not die. Your heritage will exceed throughout the times.

So my servant Levi rest; rest well, for this is your time to retire, your time to mend I opened my eyes and picked up my pen. For as John, I am compelled to share the vision and this word from on high, that Levi A. Thompson is at rest; he is all right.

So weep now, but not for too long for this male servant's life is written in the sun. The memories are not there to be stored as a thought, but are to be used as a lesson, put into livable action. I heard the word that a loved-one has gone, but you're still here and with God's help you must press on!!

By Lynette Naomi Gilbert,
© 4/27/2008

May God's blessings be upon you as you endeavor to serve Him. Live your life - everyday with purpose. My continual hope is that the statement of your life and ministry moves beyond you and your human limitations and that by God's divine intervention, you replenish the earth through the life cycle of your never ending ministry.

ASSESSMENT/STUDY QUESTIONS:
1. Why is the importance of reproduction in the ministry life cycle?
2. When should a person seek to be replenished and how?

Of the conditions mentioned in the final assessment, which one most closely applies to you and why? If none apply, where do you see yourselves in ministry? Please explain?

Appendix

Additional Resources

Bible Gateway http://www.biblegateway.com

David Baskerville, *Music Business Handbook and Career Guide* (9th Ed.)—*The New Music Business*

Donald Passman, *All You Need to Know About the Music Business* (6th Ed.)

Geoffrey Hull, Richard Strasser, The Music Business and Recording Industry ISBN 978-0-415-87561-5 © 2007

Peter F. Drucker, *Managing for the Future* (New York: Truman Talley Books, 1992),

Register of Copyrights, Library of Congress, Washington, DC 20559-6000; forms hotline is (202) 707-9100; fax on demand (not forms but other information) (202) 707-2600; Internet address is http://lcweb.loc.gov/copyright/copy1.html

Richard L. Daft, *Management* (New York: Dryden Press, 1988),53-55; R. Wayne Mondy and Shane R. Premeaux, *Management Concepts Practices and Skills*, 6th Ed. (Boston: Allyn & Bacon, 1993), 36-38.

William Krasilovsky and Sidney Shemel, *This Business of Music* (10th Ed.)

www.ingramcontent.com/pod-product-compliance
Lightning Source LLC
Chambersburg PA
CBHW022110160426
43198CB00008B/426